AND PRETEND

By
Pamela Conn Beall and
Susan Hagen Nipp

Illustrated by
Nancy Spence Klein

PSS!
PRICE STERN SLOAN

To our children—
May their imaginations continue to serve them well.

Special thanks to the Wee Singers:
Kiah Beehler, Aaron Comfort, Beth Dyer,
Sarah Dyer, Jay Miller,
Karley Molzahn, Marcus Varner,
and to our musical producers and arrangers,
Barry Hagen and Mauri Macy

Printed on recycled paper

Cover illustration copyright © 2002 by Liisa Chauncy Guida

Typesetting and engraving by Sherry Macy
Lines, Curves & Dots Graphics

PREFACE

Children love to pretend. Whether it's playing dress up, flying like an airplane, or galloping like a horse, imaginations soar when a child "becomes" the object of his pretending. This freedom of creativity contributes to emotional and intellectual development as the child expresses himself and continually makes decisions while pretending.

Wee Sing and Pretend expands the realm of pretend through the medium of music. A variety of tempos, dynamics, instrumentation, and sound effects create many different moods that encourage creative expression. Musical selections range from traditional songs such as "Row, Row, Row Your Boat" to original songs about dinosaurs. Classical favorites like "Carnival of the Animals," "Flight of the Bumblebee," and the "William Tell Overture" add another dimension to the pretending. We have included a wide variety of subjects familiar to children from animals to clowns to race cars.

Beyond the joy of pretending, children will become familiar with classical music, learn lyrics to new songs, experiment with different types of movement, and creatively determine how to enact each pretend.

We have had fun pretending while writing this book. In addition, we have found it to be a great source of exercise. We hope you'll join your children in the world of pretend and find great joy as you watch their imaginations take flight.

Pam Beall
Susan Nipp

TABLE OF CONTENTS

ANIMALS

TOYS

MUSIC

Animals

LION

The lion is the King of Beasts,
He roams across the land,
With head held high, he gives a roar,
He's awesome and he's grand.

WILD HORSES

Up and down and all around,
The wild horses race,
With dashing hooves and flying manes,
They love this game of chase.

TURTLE

Although you think the turtle's slow,
He's looking at the scenery,
And sometimes he will slow down more
To stop and eat the greenery.

ELEPHANT

The huge, enormous elephant
Moves slowly in the sun,
He dunks his trunk to drink from lakes
And rolls in mud for fun.

KANGAROO

The Australian kangaroo is happy
Hopping through the day,
He hops, then stops to eat and rest,
Then travels on his way.

FISH

Shimmering, glimmering, under the sea,
The fish swim quietly,
With flickering fins and swishing tails
And mouths that move silently.

BIRDS

Flitting and flying, soaring and gliding,
Birds are everywhere.
They zip and they zoom, they dart and they dive,
Beautiful birds in the air.

Susan Nipp

(Saint-Saëns: *Carnival of the Animals*—1886)

Dinosaurs

I'm a huge brontosaurus dinosaur, stomping around on the ground!

BRONTOSAURUS

Nancy Klein   Nancy Klein

Feel the ground shake, see the trees quake,

What is it, does an - y - bod - y know?

Huge, e - nor - mous bron - to - sau - rus,

Caus-ing earth-quakes ev - 'ry-where he goes.

I can soar high in the sky. I'm a big flying reptile, a pteranodon!

PTERANODON

Nancy Klein   *Nancy Klein*

The great, wide pter - an - o - don soar - ing so high,

He'd glide with the wind and then dive from the

sky, He'd scoop up a fish as he skimmed o'er the

sea, This great fly - ing rep - tile was free as could be.

I'm a dinosaur with long legs and I can run very fast. I'm an ornithomimus!

ORNITHOMIMUS
(Bird Imitator)

Susan Nipp, Pam Beall

Mexican Folk Tune

Or-ni-tho-mi-mus, or-ni-tho-mi-mus,

He's an "Os-trich Di-no-saur,"

Or-ni-tho-mi-mus, or-ni-tho-mi-mus,

Guess what his long legs were for.

Run-ning, run-ning, run-ning, run-ning,

C7

Run-ning, run-ning, run-ning, run-ning,

Run-ning, run-ning, run-ning, run-ning,

F

That's what his long legs were for.

MIKEY THE MONKEY

Susan Nipp   *Susan Nipp*

1. Mik-ey the mon-key swings on the branch-es,

Mik-ey the mon-key swings on the branch-es,

Mik-ey the mon-key swings on the branch-es,

Mik-ey the mon-key jumps to the ground.

2. Mikey the monkey peels a banana...
   Mikey the monkey eats it all gone.

3. Mikey the monkey scratches his fleas...
   Mikey the monkey shakes them all off.

4. Mikey the monkey makes funny faces...
   Mikey the monkey scampers away.

12

THE LITTLE CATERPILLAR

Pam Beall   *Pam Beall*

1. The lit - tle cat - er - pil - lar inched his

way a-cross the branch, Nib-bling leaves a-long the

way, He looked up in the sky and saw a

pret - ty but - ter - fly, And he

won - dered if he'd fly some day.

Chorus

But - ter - fly, but - ter - fly, how you

fly so free, But - ter - fly, but - ter -

fly, wish that I could be A - ble to

fly so high up in the sky Like a

beau - ti - ful but - ter - fly._____

2. The little caterpillar formed a cozy little shell,
   Then curled up with a sleepy sigh.
   He dreamed sweet dreams of butterflies
     and hoped that someday soon
   He'd be flying high up in the sky.

3. The little caterpillar woke and wriggled from his shell,
   Feeling something very new.
   And then he saw his pretty wings as they began to flutter,
   And up into the sky he flew.
     (Chorus)
   Butterfly, butterfly, now I fly so free,
   Butterfly, butterfly, can't believe it's me,
   Able to fly so high up in the sky,
   I'm a beautiful butterfly.

THE BUMBLEBEE

The bumblebee keeps busy
Drinking nectar from the flowers,
It's yellow and black from front to back,
And hums for hours and hours.

Susan Nipp

(Rimsky-Korsakov: *Flight of the Bumblebee* — 1900)

BUGS

Susan Nipp   *Traditional*

1. The green grass-hop-per hopped and hopped on

top the pop-corn crop, Oh, the green grass-hop-per

hopped and hopped on top the pop-corn crop, The

green grass - hop - per hopped and hopped on

18

top the pop-corn crop, Oh, the green grass-hop-per

hopped and hopped on top the pop-corn crop.

2. The inchworm arched and inched his way along the brownish branch...

3. The dragonfly flew fast for fun while flitting on four wings...

4. The red ants hurried as they scurried all around the ground...

5. I sat on the ants and got ants in my pants and ran fast to get rid of the ants...

ANIMAL ACTION

Move to the rhythm, move to the beat,
Move your body and move your feet.

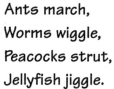

Birds fly,
Rabbits hop,
Fish swim,
Frogs kerplop!

Ants march,
Worms wiggle,
Peacocks strut,
Jellyfish jiggle.

Move to the rhythm, move to the beat,
Move your body and move your feet.

Monkeys swing,
Lions stalk,
Eagles soar,
People walk.

Penguins waddle,
Kangaroos jump,
Mice scurry,
Camels galumph.

Move to the rhythm, move to the beat,
Move your body and move your feet.

Pam Beall

It's a beautiful, sunny day. Let's get in the boat and row down the stream.

ROW, ROW, ROW YOUR BOAT

E. O. Lyte

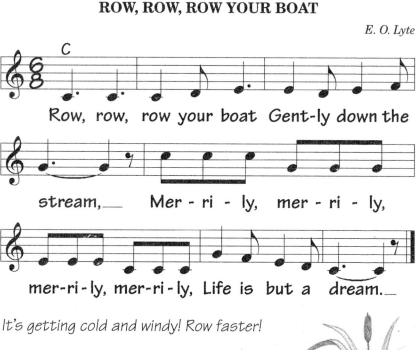

Row, row, row your boat Gent-ly down the stream,___ Mer - ri - ly, mer - ri - ly, mer-ri - ly, mer-ri - ly, Life is but a dream.___

It's getting cold and windy! Row faster!

Row, row, row your boat
Gently down the stream,
Merrily, merrily, merrily, merrily,
Life is but a dream.

There are rain clouds ahead! We need to find shelter. Row even faster!

Row, row, row your boat
Gently down the stream,
Merrily, merrily, merrily, merrily,
Life is but a dream.

It's raining! It's pouring!

Row to shore!

Jump out of the boat!

Tie up the boat!

Run for cover!

Whew!

MOTORCYCLE

Susan Nipp   Susan Nipp

Hop on, on my mo-tor-cy-cle, Fire up,

let's go, We're off on my mo-tor-cy-cle,

We're off, let's hit the road.

Rid - in' on my mo - tor - cy - cle,

Ab

rid - in' on my mo - tor - cy - cle,

Fm   G7   Cm

Rid-in' on my mo-tor-cy-cle, rid-in' down the road.

Cm

Rid - in',   rid - in',

Fm   G7   Cm

Rid-in' on my mo-tor-cy-cle, rid-in' down the road.

All aboard! Let's go, Little Blue Engine.

LITTLE BLUE ENGINE

Susan Nipp   Susan Nipp

1. "Lit - tle Blue En - gine, Lit - tle Blue En - gine,"

called the lit - tle toys,   "O - ver the moun - tain,

there's a pa - rade for all the girls and boys.

Can you pull us o - ver the top and down the oth - er

side?"   "I'll   do   my   best," said the

Lit - tle Blue En - gine. "Hold on for the ride."

"I think I can, I think I can," the Lit - tle Blue En - gine

huffed, "I think I can, I think I can," the

Lit-tle Blue En-gine puffed, "I think I can, I think I can," the Lit-tle Blue En-gine tugged. "I think I can, I think I can," the Lit-tle Blue En-gine chugged.

2. The toys began to hope and smile as the train moved down the track,
   "I'm not very big, but I can try," the engine smiled back.
   Faster, faster, the engine climbed up to the mountain top,
   The toys all cheered as the Little Blue Engine said, "I will not stop."

   (Chorus)

3. The Little Blue Engine pulled the train with all her strength and will,
   With one big puff she reached the top, then started down the hill,
   "Hurray, hurray, we knew you could," the little toy band cried,
   "We'll make it to the big parade 'cuz the Little Blue Engine tried."

   (Chorus)

"I thought I could, I thought I could,..."

AIRPLANE

Susan Nipp   *Susan Nipp*

Sit-ting in the cock-pit of my air-plane, ___

Start-ing en-gine num-ber one, ___ Start-ing en-gine

num-ber two, ___ Rum - ble, _____

Mov-ing down the run-way, fast-er and fast-er,

Mov-ing down the run-way, fast-er and fast-er,

Lift off!   Fly - ing, fly - ing up in the

sky,   Fly - ing,   fly - ing,   I'm up   so   high,

Lift-ing up,   div - ing down,   Bank-ing left,

bank-ing right,   Fly - ing, fly - ing, high in the sky.

Run - way in   sight,   flaps   down,_____

Glid - ing,   glid - ing,   glid - ing   down.

Glid - ing,   glid - ing,   now it's touch - down.

RACE CAR

Susan Nipp　　　　　　　　　　　　　　　　　　　　*Traditional*

1. Driv-in' down the race-track just as fast as I can,—
Fast as I can,— fast as I can,—
Driv-in' down the race-track just as fast as I can,—
How I want to win this race.

30

Turn to the left!

Turn to the right!

Slam on the brakes!

Whoa, I'm spinning around!

Whew! I'm back on the track and racing for the finish line!

2. Drivin' down the racetrack just as fast as I can,
Fast as I can, fast as I can,
Drivin' down the racetrack just as fast as I can,
It's the checkered flag, *I WIN!*

THE LAND OF SILLY

Susan Nipp, Adapted

Traditional

I love to walk in the Land of Sil-ly, where

I can be so sil-ly, wil-ly-nil-ly, With a

hob-a-lob-a-loo and a wil-la-bil-la-bee, With a

bib - a - lob - a - loo   bo   beel.

F

Shool,   shool,   shool I   rool,

C7

F   C7

Shool I shag-a-rack shool-a-bob-a-loo, In the

F   B♭

and of Sil-ly with a nil-ly wil-ly we, With a

F   C7   F

bib - a - lob - a - loo bo   beel.

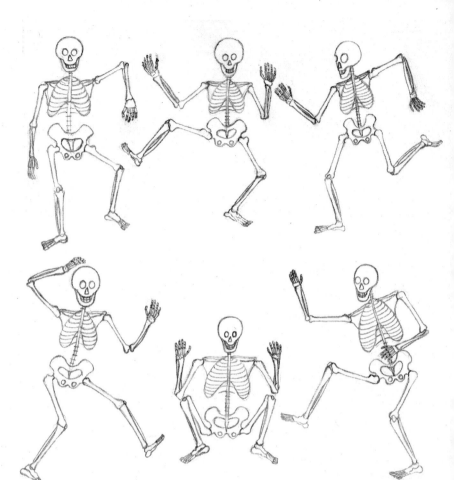

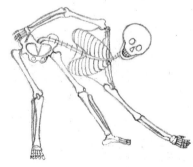

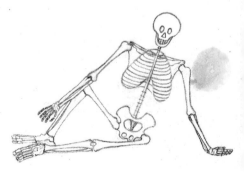

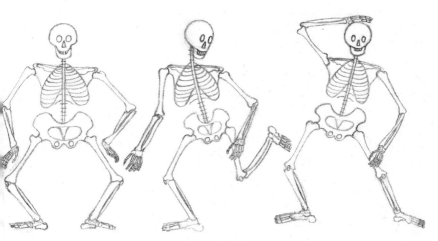

BONES

My bones make up my skeleton,
Which is the frame of me,
And though you cannot see them,
My bones move easily.

For I can leap and twist and creep
And run and sway and jiggle
And bend and slide and hop and glide
And bounce and roll and wiggle.

Susan Nipp

(Saint-Saëns: *Danse Macabre* — 1875)

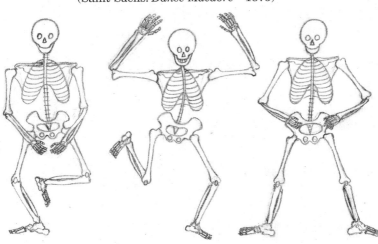

I'M A CLOWN

Susan Nipp

Traditional

1. I'm a clown! Honk! Honk!

I'm a clown! Honk! Honk!

Jug-gl-ing, jug-gl-ing, toss the balls,

Strug-gl-ing, strug-gl-ing as they fall,

Tum-bl-ing, stum-bl-ing, fum-bl-ing, mum-bl-ing,

Catch   the   balls.

2. I'm a clown! *Honk! Honk!*
   I'm a clown! *Honk! Honk!*
   Somersault, somersault, over I go,
   Over and round on the ground I go,
   Down on the ground going over and round
   From my head to toe.

3. I'm a clown! *Honk! Honk!*
   I'm a clown! *Honk! Honk!*
   Balancing, balancing on the wire,
   High on the wire, so I must not tire,
   Tipping and dipping and slipping and tripping while
   On the wire.

The Cowboy

I'm a cowboy and this is my horse, Old Paint.

All right, Old Paint, I'll brush you down a bit.

Here, have some oats.

Now, I'll put on the saddle.

Hold still, boy, while I get on.

All right, Old Paint, let's start walking down the trail.

OLD TEXAS

Traditional

1. I'm goin' to leave ____ old __ Tex-as now, They've got no use _____ for the long - horned cow. _____

2. The hard, hard ground will be my bed,
   And the saddle seat will hold my head.

38

Okay, Old Paint, let's trot along a bit faster.

THE OLD CHISHOLM TRAIL

Traditional

1. Oh, come a-long boys and lis-ten to my tale,
I'll tell you of my trou-bles on the old Chis-holm Trail,

Chorus
Sing-in' ki-yi yip-pi yip-pi yay, yip-pi yay!
Sing-in' ki-yi yip-pi yip-pi yay! ____

2. I'm up in the mornin' before daylight,
   And before I sleep, the moon shines bright.

   (Chorus)

Ready, Old Paint? Let's gallop!

(Rossini: *William Tell Overture* — 1829)

39

THE LAND OF SLOW MOTION

Susan Nipp   *Susan Nipp*

Verse   F   G7   C

1. I'm wak-ing up in the Land of Slow Mo-tion,

G7   C

Land of Slow Mo-tion, Land of Slow Mo-tion, I'm

F   G7   C

wak-ing up in the Land of Slow Mo-tion and

Dm   G7   C

I   can   bare - ly   move.

(Chorus—spoken slowly)
I get out of bed...
And brush my teeth...
Put on my clothes...
And have something to eat...

I run outside...
And play catch with my brother...
I ride my bike...
Then swim with my sister...

I jump over rocks...
And climb a tree...
Then run back home...
And eat with my family...

I put on my pajamas...
And brush my teeth...
I go to bed...
And fall right to sleep.

(Verse—quickly)

2. I'm waking up in the Land of Fast Motion,
   Land of Fast Motion, Land of Fast Motion,
   I'm waking up in the Land of Fast Motion,
   And I can hardly stop.

   (Repeat chorus—spoken quickly)

Around the house, there are all kinds of things that move. Can you move like they do?

OH, WHEN

Susan Nipp, Pam Beall

Traditional

1. Oh, when the clothes wash in the wash-er, Oh, when the clothes wash in the wash-er, Oh, how they slish and slosh in the wash-er,_____ When the clothes wash in the wash-er.

2. Oh, when the clothes dry in the dryer,
   Oh, when the clothes dry in the dryer,
   Oh, how they tumble, tumble, tumble in the dryer,
   When the clothes dry in the dryer.

3. Oh, when the juice twirls in the blender,
   Oh, when the juice twirls in the blender,
   Oh, how it twirls and swirls in the blender,
   When the juice twirls in the blender.

4. Oh, when the corn pops in the popper,
   Oh, when the corn pops in the popper,
   Oh, how it pops and pops in the popper,
   When the corn pops in the popper.

What is that in the middle of the sidewalk?

A ROCK BLOCKS THE WALK

Susan Nipp   *Traditional*

D

1. A rock blocks the walk, A

rock blocks the walk. How can I

A7   D

move the thing? A rock blocks the walk.

2. I push on the rock,
   I push on the rock.
   How can I move the thing?
   I push on the rock.

44

3. I pull on the rock,
   I pull on the rock.
   How can I move the thing?
   I pull on the rock.

4. I walk round the rock,
   I walk round the rock,
   I cannot move the thing,
   So, I walk round the rock on the block.

A WALK THROUGH THE FOREST

One day little Chipper Chipmunk peeked through my window. He blinked at me as though asking me to play. I hurried outside to find him and he began to scamper away.

We ran through the meadow.
(Vivaldi: *Flute Concerto in G Minor, "LaNotte," Allegro* — 1731)

We skipped down the forest trail.
(Rimsky-Korsakov: *Alborado* from *Cappriccio Espagnol* — 1892

We balanced on a log over the rushing stream.
(Sibelius: *Finlandia* — 1899)

We tiptoed past sleeping Mr. Porcupine.
(Bach: *Air on G String* from *Suite No. 3 in D* — 1727)

We hopped around the trees with Missy Rabbit.
(Tchaikovsky: *Polonaise* from *Eugene Onegin* — 1878)

We twirled with the leaves as they fell from the trees.
(Grieg: *Morning* from *Peer Gynt* — 1876)

We helped the ants carry their heavy picnic baskets slowly to the sandy beach.
(Elgar: *Pomp and Circumstance, March No. 1* — 1901)

After the picnic, we played and danced with the ants.
(Bizet: *Les Toreadors* from *Carmen* — 1875)

We waved good-bye to the ants and continued down the path.

We came to a dark tunnel and crawled through it.
(Handel: *Largo* from *Xerxes* — 1734)

I came out of the tunnel and couldn't find Chipper. What happened? I went to look for him.
(Beethoven: *Symphony No. 5, 1st Movement* — 1885)

Hooray! I found him playfully hiding behind a bush. We laughed and called our forest friends to join us as we danced wildly.
(J. Strauss II: *Tritsch Tratsch Polka* — 1858)

As we thought about our wonderful day, we happily marched back home.
(Purcell: *Trumpet Tune* — 1685)

Susan Nipp

47

Inside a box, I'm scrunched up tight,
I do not move 'til the music's right.

JACK-IN-THE-BOX

Susan Nipp

Traditional

1. My name is Jack-in-the-Box, I love to hide from you, I qui-et-ly stay in-side the box, 'Til POP! I sur-prise you.

2. Down I go back into my box
   To hide again from you,
   I quietly stay inside the box,
   'Til POP! I surprise you.

48

MY BLUE BALLOON

Susan Nipp   Susan Nipp

I have a blue bal-loon in my pock-et, I have a blue bal-loon in my pock-et, I'll show it to you, ___ It's ti-ny, that's true, ___ But it can get real-ly big.

Whoo, *(blowing)* whoo, ___ whoo, ___

whoo,_____ Whew! Tie a knot!

Oops! Watch out! Try again!

Whoo,_____ whoo,_____ whoo,_____

whoo,_____ Whew! Tie a knot!

Float-ing, float-ing, my big blue bal - loon,

Float-ing, float-ing, my big blue bal - loon,

Swirl-ing and twirl-ing and whirl-ing a-round, My

big blue bal - loon in the air._____

It's floating down! POP!

I'M A TOP

Susan Nipp

Susan Nipp

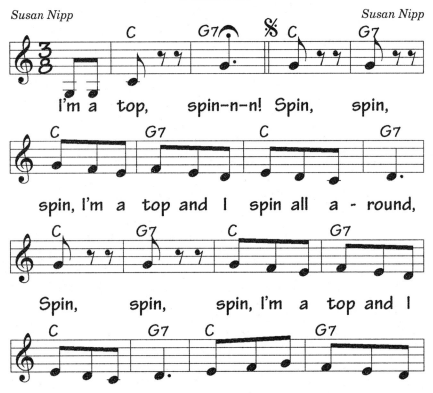

I'm a top, spin-n-n! Spin, spin,

spin, I'm a top and I spin all a - round,

Spin, spin, spin, I'm a top and I

spin all a - round, Spin-ning and spin-ning and

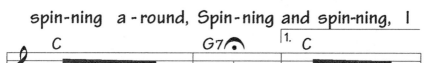

spin-ning a - round, Spin-ning and spin-ning, I

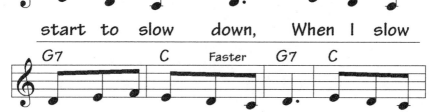

start to slow down, When I slow

down, then I start once a - gain, Fast-er and

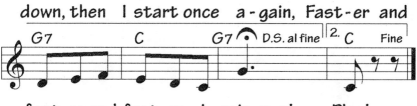

fast-er and fast-er I spin-n–n! Plop!

THE TOY SHOP AT MIDNIGHT

The toys in the toy shop are silent all day,
But when it is midnight, they all start to play.

The little tin soldier marches quite stiffly...
(Herbert: *March of the Toys* from *Babes in Toyland* — 1903)

The fluffy old rag doll flops as she walks...
(Vivaldi: *The Four Seasons, Autumn; Allegro* — 1725)

The small ballerina twirls on her toes...
(Tchaikovsky: *Waltz of the Flowers* from *The Nutcracker* — 1892)

The mechanical robot moves with a jerk...
(Debussy: *Golliwogg's Cakewalk* from *Children's Corner* — 1908)

The big, cuddly teddy bear dances quite clumsily...
(Tchaikovsky: *Piano Concerto No. 1 in B Flat minor, 1st Movement* — 1875)

But just as the sun starts to peek o'er the hill,
The toys take their places and once more are still.
(Grieg: *Morning* from *Peer Gynt* — 1876)

Susan Nipp

THE ORCHESTRA

MARCH

Attention!
March in place, 2, 3, 4!
Left, right, left, right, left, right, left!
Forward...march, 2, 3, 4,
1, 2, 3, 4!

To the left...march!

To the right...march!

To the rear...march!

Attention, 2, 3, 4,
1, 2, 3, 4,
Ready...stop!

(John Philip Sousa: *The Stars and Stripes Forever*—1897)

58

ROCK BAND

Susan Nipp   *Susan Nipp*

Rock-in' and a-roll-in' in my rock band,___

Rock-in' and a-roll-in' in my rock band,___

Rock-in' and a-roll-in' in my rock band,___

Oh,___ let's rock.___

Let's hear the 'lec-tric gui-tar,___ *(guitar)*

60

C

Let's hear the key - board __ rock, __ *(keyboard)*

F

Let's hear the drum - set __ roll, __ *(drumset)*

C

Let's hear the sax - o - phone, __ *(saxophone)*

F

Let's hear the 'lec - tric __ bass, __ *(electric bass)*

G7   D.C. al fine

Oh,   let's   rock.

INDEX

Discover the entire best-selling line of Wee Sing® books, audio, and videos

Book & Audiocassette packages

• Wee Sing Children's Songs and Fingerplays • Wee Sing and Play
• Wee Sing Silly Songs • Wee Sing Sing-Alongs
• Wee Sing for Christmas • Wee Sing Nursery Rhymes and Lullabies
• Wee Sing Bible Songs • Wee Sing America • Wee Sing Fun 'n' Folk
• Wee Sing Dinosaurs • Wee Sing Around the World
• Wee Sing More Bible Songs • Wee Sing for Baby
• Wee Sing Games, Games, Games • Wee Sing in the Car
• Wee Sing Animals, Animals, Animals • Wee Sing and Pretend
• Wee Sing 25th Anniversary Celebration • Wee Sing for Halloween

Book & CD (with FREE audiocassette) packages

• Wee Sing Children's Songs and Fingerplays • Wee Sing and Play
• Wee Sing Silly Songs • Wee Sing Sing-Alongs
• Wee Sing for Christmas • Wee Sing Nursery Rhymes and Lullabies
• Wee Sing Bible Songs • Wee Sing America • Wee Sing Fun 'n' Folk
• Wee Sing Dinosaurs • Wee Sing Around the World
• Wee Sing More Bible Songs • Wee Sing for Baby
• Wee Sing Games, Games, Games • Wee Sing in the Car
• Wee Sing Animals, Animals, Animals • Wee Sing and Pretend
• Wee Sing 25th Anniversary Celebration • Wee Sing for Halloween

Wee Sing® & Learn Book & Audiocassette packages

• Wee Sing & Learn ABC • Wee Sing & Learn 123
• Wee Sing & Learn Colors • Wee Sing & Learn Bugs
• Wee Sing & Learn Dinosaurs

Board Books

• The Hokey Pokey • Away in a Manger
• The Ten Days of Christmas • The Ants Go Marching
• If You're Happy and You Know It • Old MacDonald

Live-Action Videos

• Wee Sing Together • King Cole's Party • Grandpa's Magical Toys
• Wee Sing in Sillyville • The Best Christmas Ever!
• Wee Sing in the Big Rock Candy Mountains
• Wee Sing in the Marvelous Musical Mansion
• The Wee Sing Train • Wee Sing Under the Sea
• Animal Songs • Classic Songs for Kids • Wee Singdom

Also available

• The Wee Sing Musical Bible

**Wee Sing® products are available
wherever children's books and toys are sold.**